ART FROM PACKAGING

with projects using cardboard, plastics, foil, and tape

Gillian Chapman & Pam Robson

RSVP

RAINTREE
STECK-VAUGHN
PUBLISHERS
The Steck-Vaughn Company

Austin, Texas

SALVAGED!

Art from Fabric
Art from Packaging
Art from Paper
Art from Rocks and Shells
Art from Sand and Earth
Art from Wood

© Copyright 1997, text, Steck-Vaughn Company

Published by Raintree Steck-Vaughn Publishers, an imprint of Steck-Vaughn Company

Library of Congress Cataloging-in-Publication Data

Chapman, Gillian
Art from Packaging: with projects using cardboard, plastics, foil, and tape / Gillian Chapman & Pam Robson.
p.   cm. —(Salvaged!)
Includes index.
Summary: Instructions for making prints from bubblewrap, puppets from cardboard boxes, and other arts and crafts projects using discarded packaging.
ISBN 0-8172-4550-2
1. Packaging—Materials—Juvenile literature
2. Recycling (Waste, etc.)—Juvenile literature
3. Paper work—Juvenile literature
4. Plastic craft—Juvenile literature
5. Aluminum foil craft—Juvenile literature
[1. Handicraft. 2. Recycling—Waste.]
I. Robson, Pam. II. Title. III. Series.
TT160.C49   1997
745.58'4—dc20   96-8363

Photo Acknowledgments
Ecoscene 4b (Sally Morgan), 5t (Whatmore)
Lois Walpole 4t, 5b

Printed in Italy
1 2 3 4 5 6 7 8 9 0 0 01 00 99 98 97

Contents

Reams of Wrapping

The Importance of Packaging

In America and Europe during the nineteenth century, people did their shopping at general stores. Dry goods, such as cereals, sugar, and tea were individually weighed then packed in twists of paper and wrappings of the shopkeeper's own design.

The first mass-produced paper bags were made in Pennsylvania in 1852, but it was the production of the folding carton that revolutionized packaging. Cartons could be used to package a wide variety of products. Packaging soon became as important as the product itself.

Laundry basket made by Lois Walpole out of recycled apple juice cartons and cardboard

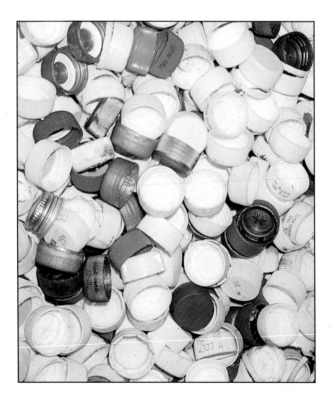

Plastic bottle tops can be used in a variety of art projects.

The Purpose of Packaging

Packaging is a term used to describe a vast range of materials and containers. Its purpose is to protect and advertise the products we purchase in our stores. Packaging becomes worthless and disposable once its contents are used. Cardboard boxes, tubes, cans, plastic tapes and wires, cartons, bottle tops, and labels are some items you can collect. They do have value, and this book makes some exciting suggestions for putting to good use packaging that might once have been considered garbage.

Aluminum cans reused as building material in Botswana, Africa

Precycling

About 30 percent of manufactured plastic is used for packaging; about half the weight of the plastic we throw away is packaging. One way to help avoid this waste is to precycle, which means to stop buying goods packaged in layers of unnecessary plastic wrappers. Buy drinks in glass bottles and aluminum cans that can be recycled.

Recycling Packaging

Aluminum cans are about 20 percent cheaper to recycle than to make and need 5 percent of the energy. In Padua a model of the Basilica Sant'Antonio has been erected using 3,250,000 cans, collected from streets and homes. In 1992, Sweden collected 787 million cans.

During World War II (1939–1945), people were asked to salvage all useful items that might otherwise have been discarded. Garbage was sorted into separate bins. Present-day recycling centers are organized in the same way. Scrap iron was claimed by the government for munitions. Even iron railings were removed, and aluminum saucepans were turned into airplanes. Modern packagers can reuse aluminum, glass paper, and cardboard. Make sure you sort your garbage and take it to your local collection center.

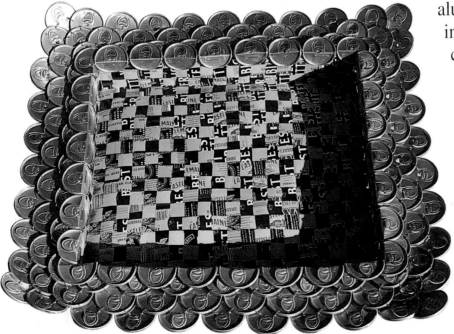

A large dish made by Lois Walpole from used cans

Printing Patterns

Printing Blocks

Printing blocks are traditionally made from wood; the harder the wood the more delicate the carving. These blocks interlock so that a repeating pattern can be accurately printed over a large area. Indian craftworkers are highly skilled at producing intricate designs printed on cotton textiles.

You can use a whole range of packaging materials to make exciting patterns. Simple printing blocks can be made from polystyrene packing. The blocks are easy to carve and shape, yet are firm enough to use many times.

Prints made with packaging

Textured Prints

To make a textured print, find a large piece of textured wrapping such as bubble wrap or corrugated cardboard. Cover this with colored ink or paint, and press gently onto a piece of plain paper. Let it dry, then carefully peel off the wrapping. It will have left a colorful, textured pattern.

This kind of print is called a monoprint. Because wrapping cannot be used again in the same way, every print is unique. With repeated printing methods, each print made from the same block is identical, and prints can be made until the block wears out.

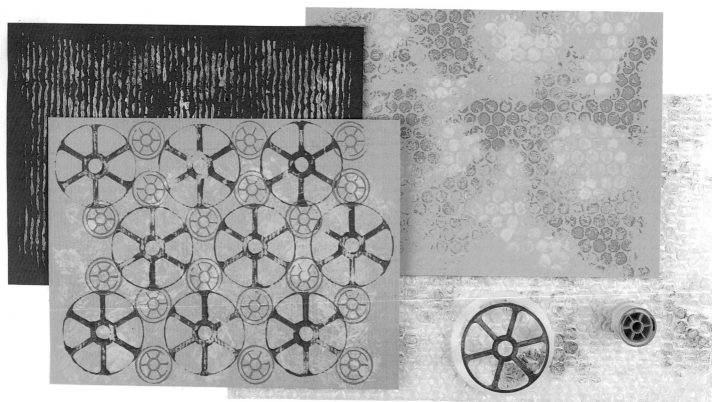

Repeating Patterns

Many items of packaging make ideal printing tools. Plastic spools and lids come in a variety of interesting shapes and sizes. See what you can find and experiment with different types. Use them to print repeating patterns and designs over the textured prints.

Printing Cans

Another way of making a repeating print involves using an empty drink can. Wind lengths of string around the can to make a pattern, and tie the string firmly in place. Cover the can in paint so that the string picks up all the color. Then slowly roll it over a strip of paper. You can see the results in the examples shown here.

Cover can with paint.

Print stripes

Printing Cans

Printed Gift Wrap

It is now common for gift wrap and greeting cards to be printed on recycled paper. By printing your own papers, you are being environmentally aware and avoiding further waste. You can produce unusual designs for special occasions.

Printed Pictures

A portfolio is a useful storage container for your prints. They can also be displayed in frames made from recycled materials. In this way you create a completely "salvaged" work of art.

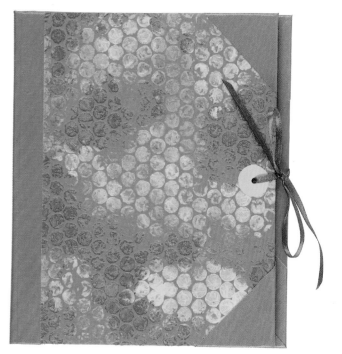

Finished portfolio

Place strong tape diagonally across the corners of the portfolio covers.

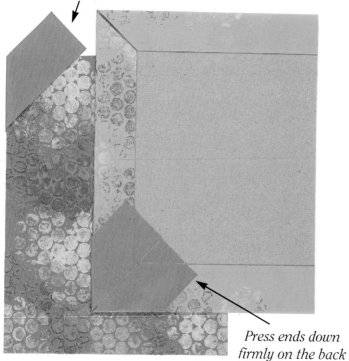

Press ends down firmly on the back of the cardboard.

Taping the corners of the portfolio

Making a Portfolio

The size of the portfolio you make will depend upon the size of your artwork. The measurements given here are for a portfolio designed to store 16 inch by 22.5 inch prints.

Cut two large pieces of scrap cardboard 24 inches by 17.5 inches. Cover the outsides using your own printed papers, taping across the corners for extra protection. Cover the inside of both pieces, again using printed papers.

Tape the covers together along the longest sides. Make flaps to fit inside one of the covers, and glue them in place to hold the artwork. Cut slots in the two covers and thread tape through.

Picture Frames

To make a frame to fit a particular piece of artwork, you will need to work to precise measurements. Cut a frame from stiff cardboard, making the window opening 0.75 inches smaller than the print. The width of the frame should be 2.5 inches all round. Make a backing cardboard the same size as the frame.

The frames shown here have been covered with squares of corrugated cardboard, crumpled foil, and colored twine. Decorate the frame and paint it first before attaching the backing cardboard. Finally, mount your print between them. Glue a strip of cardboard to the back of the frame to give it support.

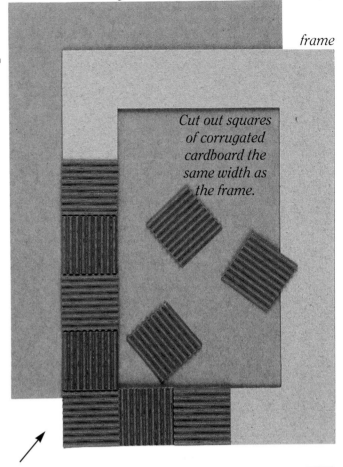

backing card

frame

Cut out squares of corrugated cardboard the same width as the frame.

Build up a pattern along the frame.

Making picture frames

finished frames

back view

9

Plastic Art

Plastics

Some plastics are biodegradable, but most are not. It is possible to melt down certain plastic items for reuse in another form. The rest must be burned, causing toxic fumes, or tipped into landfall sites, creating methane gas, which can be dangerous. Soft-drink bottles made from polyethylene terephthalate (PET) can be melted down and turned into a cottony fiber. This can be used as insulation or even for new carpets.

Plastic Products

Look around you and see how much plastic has been used and discarded. Start to make a plastic collection that can be used for projects. Plastic bags, wrappings, tapes, and twines are perfect for craftwork—the more colorful they are, the better.

Woven Mats

You can make colorful mats from plastic tapes and twine woven and twisted around cardboard shapes. Cut out the mat shape from a piece of scrap cardboard and make notches along the two opposite sides. Wind thin, flexible plastic twine or wire around the notches, as shown here. Then weave across the twine with thicker tapes. The finished mats are both attractive and practical.

Make notches along two sides of the cardboard.

Secure lengths of colored twine with tape.

making the frame

finished mat

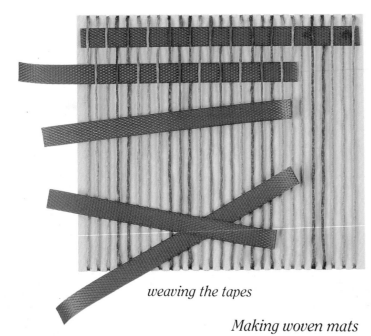

weaving the tapes

Making woven mats

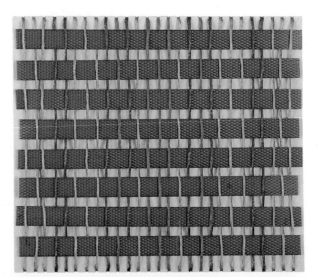

Purposeful Projects

In the 1950s, the mass production of flexible plastic made it ideal for packaging. It was hygienic, cheap, and malleable. Until recently, manufacturers used it without any thought for the environmental consequences.

By using nonrecyclable packaging for purposeful projects, you can make a positive contribution toward reducing the large amount of garbage, and help conserve Earth's natural resources.

Plastic picture

Plastic twine and packaging

Plastic Pictures

Weaving a picture out of plastic materials makes use of a wide range of disposable packaging. First, you will need to draw a simple picture on paper. Then, place a piece of plastic netting over the top. Weave different colored lengths of plastic in and out of the netting, following the design behind the mesh. Choose colors and textures that suit the subject. Mount the finished picture onto a plastic backing.

Woven Baskets

Natural Baskets

Palm fronds were the first fans. Whole leaves were the first umbrellas. The first baskets were woven using readily available natural materials, usually rattans. Baskets can be made by weaving or coiling. Werregue baskets, made by the Waunana people of Colombia, were so tightly coiled and stitched that water could be carried in them. Today the Waunana use plastic to make their baskets, while the original baskets fetch high prices among collectors.

Modern Baskets

Basket makers, like Great Britain's Lois Walpole, who live and work in an urban environment, have developed the art of weaving using modern packaging materials. Cardboard, netting, and plastic are woven into colorful, practical baskets using traditional methods. Here are two baskets you can make using modern materials.

Banana-Shaped Basket

This simple basket is made from 6 strips of strong cardboard 1.25 inches by 12 inches. Paint the cardboard first, using bright PVA paints, and let it dry before cutting. Then, punch holes in the strips, 1.25 inches from each end. Assemble the strips and fasten them at one end with a large paper fastener. Fan out the basket and weave colored twine in and out of the strips before fastening the other end.

strips attached with one fastener

basket shape formed with two fasteners

Loosely weave twine between the strips before securing the second fastener.

Assemble basket and tighten the twine to keep the shape.

Making a banana-shaped basket

Woven Plate

To make the plate, find some cardboard that is both strong and flexible. Paint it with PVA colors and cut it into 1.25 inch by 12 inch strips. Weave the strips together, as shown here, holding them in place with pegs.

When the weaving is the correct shape and size, trim any surplus lengths of cardboard. Staple the woven strips in position. Measure around the edge of the plate and cut a 3-inch cardboard strip to the same length. Fold this in half lengthwise and bind it around the edge, holding it in place with pegs. Sew this strip to the plate using colored wire or twine with a blunt-ended needle.

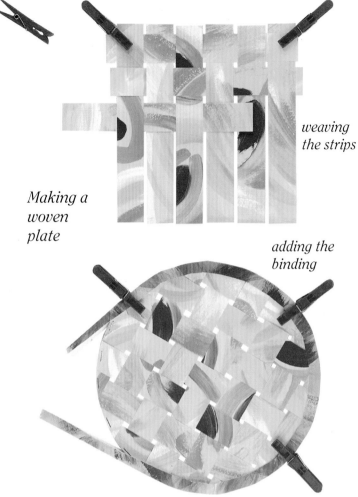

Making a woven plate

weaving the strips

adding the binding

Finished plates and basket

Woven Boxes

Cardboard Cities

In some parts of the world, there are shantytowns built on the edges of large cities. Here poor people use materials, like cardboard, that many others would call waste. In other places, the homeless sleep under bridges and in doorways protected by cardboard boxes. The insulating properties of the cardboard help keep these people warm.

Cardboard Boxes

The production of a cardboard box that could be folded from one piece of flat cardboard revolutionized packaging in the 1850s. Cartons became cheap and easy to produce, but were also disposable. Modern society has become dependent on the cardboard box to package almost everything we buy.

Look at the cartons and boxes used in stores and supermarkets to package food products, toiletries, and many other items. Many have interesting graphics and labeling. A great deal of time and money goes into their design, yet they are rarely reused, and most of them are thrown away.

Three-Dimensional Weaving

A cardboard box can be used again as a structure for a three-dimensional weaving. Find a suitable box and seal the top and bottom with tape. Paint all the sides to cover up any printing and cut a series of notches in the edges. Wind colored plastic twine around these notches. You can then interweave more twine and tape, forming a three-dimensional woven cube.

Painted box with weaving

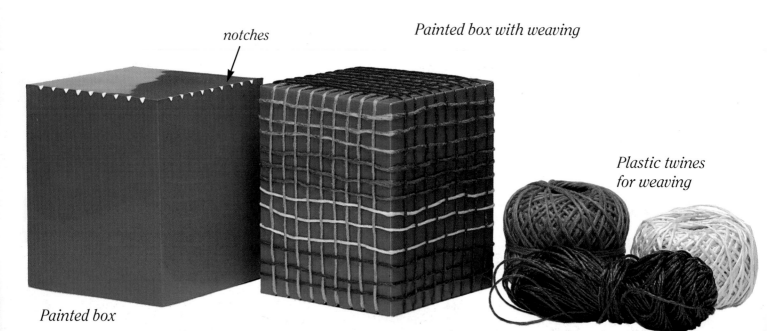

notches

Plastic twines for weaving

Painted box

Woven Boxes

These boxes are woven from strips of flexible cardboard. Use any scrap cardboard—cereal boxes are ideal—painting them first to disguise the surface.

Cut 10 cardboard strips 1.25 inches by 17.5 inches and weave them into place as shown, forming the base of the box. Bend each cardboard strip so that it forms a right angle to the base. Cut five strips 1.25 inches by 27 inches and weave them through these strips, forming the sides of the box. Finish off by tucking the ends inside the box.

Finishing Off

Cut a strip of cardboard 2.5 inches by 25 inches and crease it along the center. Fold it over the top edge of the box. Sew the strip into place with colored twine, using a large blunt-ended needle and blanket stitch. To make a lid, use 10 cardboard strips 1.25 inches by 9.5 inches and follow the weaving instructions for the box.

Weaving a box

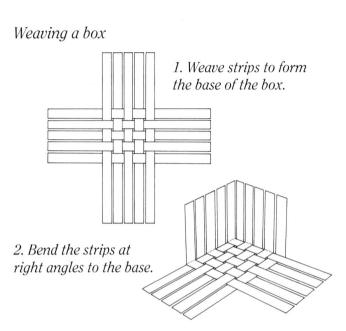

1. Weave strips to form the base of the box.

2. Bend the strips at right angles to the base.

3. Weave strips around the box to form the sides.

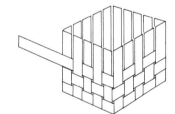

Finished woven box and lid

Figures from Foil

Packaging with Foil

Between 1910 and 1920, two new materials were introduced to the packaging industry. They were aluminum foil and cellophane. They were used to wrap many different products, especially food, keeping it clean and fresh. Because it is such a practical material, aluminum is used extensively today to package a great variety of foods, from fresh and frozen items to carbonated drinks.

Aluminum is an attractive material for packaging because it is lightweight and malleable. It is also an easy material to recycle. Seattle, Washington, has introduced a recycling program that recovers 45 percent of its waste. From 1.7 million tons of aluminum thrown away in a year, 1 million tons are recycled. Cans are 20 percent cheaper to make from recycled aluminum, and the process requires only 5 percent of the energy.

Working with Foil

Foil is a soft material, so it is easy to shape. Collect together some discarded foil containers, such as plates or small pie dishes; make sure they are cleaned thoroughly before using them. Foil can be cut with scissors, but be careful of any sharp edges.

Making Foil Figures

Find several clean foil plates of different shapes and sizes. A large, round plate can make the base for a foil figure. Draw patterns onto the foil with a ballpoint pen. The pen will leave impressions in the soft foil. Cut out sections and shapes from the smaller plates for features and staple them to the base. Finally, cut a slot in the base of a small foil dish, and use it as a stand for the foil figure.

Foil figure

Making a Foil Hanging

To make a foil picture, first cut a base out of thin cardboard, about 12 inches square. Cut a piece of foil, about 2 inches larger than the cardboard. Crinkle the foil and then carefully flatten it. Using PVA, glue it to the cardboard, overlapping the sides as shown here.

Find a clean foil plate that is about 8 inches in diameter. Draw a face design on the plate, using a ballpoint pen to make patterns. Cut out the eyes and mouth with scissors. Glue the face to the foil backing.

Covering card with foil

Coloring Foil

To give the background foil a burnished, metallic look, try painting it with colored ink. Be careful not to flatten the crinkled texture. Tape two pull tabs to the back of the picture and use them to pin it to the wall.

Making a foil face

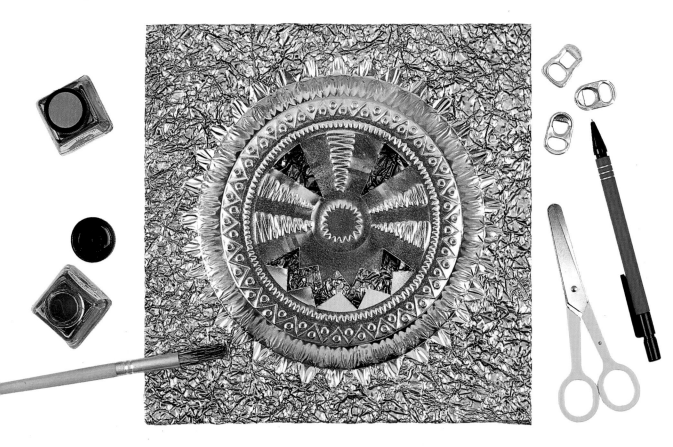

Junk Art

Found Objects

Artists are often inspired by the shape of a particular object when creating a work of art. Picasso used a toy car to shape the head on his baboon sculpture. He created many sculptures out of found objects and then cast them in bronze. He also made a bull's head out of a bicycle saddle and a pair of handlebars.

Junk figures

A Second Chance

Unnecessary packaging adds to the mountains of garbage accumulating in our throwaway world. Products are packaged in many ways, but paper containers coated with wax or lined with plastic cannot be recycled. It is these items that we need to reuse.

Give all packaging a second chance. Can an empty container or bottle be used again in a practical way, or does it suggest to you a particular figure or shape? You may be able to use it in a fun way. Look at the ideas here and try to think up some of your own.

Junk Figures

These figures have been made from a range of plastic bottles and containers. Paint the containers first with acrylic paints and then glue scraps of colored paper, tape, and fabric to them. Half fill them with sand or gravel and use them as bowling pins.

Tubular Figures

Cardboard tubes and rolls are very strong structures that are used to support many household products. Here is a way to put them to good use.

Collect together a selection of different sized tubes. Large tubes will be needed for the head and body, with smaller diameter tubes for the neck, arms, and legs. Paint the tubes or cover them in colored wrapping paper before assembling the figures.

Using a large needle, make holes in the tubes, as shown in the diagram. Then thread stiff wire through the holes to make the joints, securing each end with a loop.

Different cardboard tubes

Making tubular figures

Thread stiff wire through holes to make joints.

Attach cardboard hands and feet to the figures.

19

Plant Pots

Make drainage holes in plastic containers.

Growing

Propagating flowers and vegetables from seeds or cuttings makes a very purposeful and satisfying occupation. Plastic containers are ideal to use as plant pots and are now widely used by gardeners as a cheaper alternative to terra cotta. All the containers you need for growing seeds and rooting cuttings can be recycled from everyday household containers.

Choosing Containers

Plastic yogurt, ice cream, and margarine containers can all be used as plant pots for young seedlings. Larger plastic or foil food trays are ideal for sowing small seeds. However, all these containers must be thoroughly washed before reusing, and if plants are to grow, the containers must have adequate drainage holes.

Collect suitable containers and seeds. If you do not have a garden, you can grow seeds successfully on a window ledge. It is also easy to propagate house plants from cuttings. Keep a record of their growth in a journal.

Seedlings and cuttings growing in plastic containers

Notebook to record plant growth

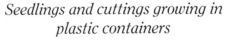

26th. April
Planted cuttings —
Spider plant, cactus
& succulents
Seedlings —
Mustard & cress
1cm tall.

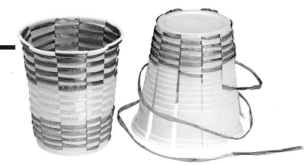

Woven pots

Decorated pots

Decorating Pots

Containers can be used just as they are once they have been washed. However, you can make them more decorative. Cut an odd number of slits in the sides and weave lengths of colored tapes in and out or cover them with colored plastic twine. Attach the twine to the pots with strips of double-sided clear tape.

Bottle Gardens

Plants growing in bottles create their own ecosystem and, once watered, will need little attention. You will need a large, clear bottle (a used storage jar is ideal). Put a 1.5-inch layer of gravel in the bottom of the jar, with a 4-inch layer of soil on top. Find out which plants grow well in a damp atmosphere and plant them in the bottle. When you next use disposable plastic knives and spoons, take them home and wash them. They make ideal tools for pot gardening. Use a plastic bottle as a watering can.

Bottle garden

Bottle garden tools

Musical Junk

Early Instruments

The first musical instruments were made from natural materials—the resonance of wood makes it an ideal material for drums. Seeds inside gourds make rattles and shakers. People have always used whatever materials were available to make music. You can create a whole orchestra of sounds by using packaging and junk materials that might otherwise be thrown away.

Many of the instruments featured on this page have their origins in the distant past. Music has always been a source of pleasure, as well as an important means of communication. Much African music is based on speech. The pitch of African "talking" drums imitates the natural sounds of the language.

Junk Drums and Shakers

Experiment with a selection of plastic, tin, and cardboard containers. Each will give a different sound if struck like a drum. If the same containers are filled with dry materials like seeds or sand, you will hear a whole range of new sounds when you shake them. To make a drum, cut off the end of a large balloon and stretch it over the open container, taping it firmly in place. Decorate the drums and shakers with colored cardboard, tape, and stickers.

*Dried materials
for shakers*

Container drums

Shakers

*Decorate with colored
cardboard, tape, and
stickers.*

Bottle top castanets

Rattles, Tambourines, and Castanets

Rattles are the simplest musical instrument and are found worldwide. In Kenya, rattles like the one shown here, are made from bottle tops threaded onto a wire loop. Castanets and tambourines are favorite instruments to accompany dancers. Metal or plastic lids attached to flexible cardboard make excellent castanets. The tambourine is made from two foil dishes stapled together and decorated with ribbons and bells.

Bottle top rattle

Plastic Didgeridoo

The didgeridoo is a traditional Aboriginal instrument. It is used in rituals to communicate with ancestors. This music is a series of almost continuous notes. Aboriginal musicians have developed the special breathing skills needed to make the familiar sounds. This didgeridoo is made from a three-foot length of plastic or cardboard tubing, and it will amplify humming sounds.

Tambourine

Didgeridoo

Decorate with colored tape and stickers.

Puppets from Packaging

Shadow Puppets

The first puppets were made in Asia, where they were used to bring to life ancient myths and legends. Cambodia, Thailand, Malaysia, and Bali have long-established shadow puppet traditions. The grotesquely fantastic shadow puppets of Java are perhaps the most splendid. Jointed puppets are manipulated by a series of long rods that keep the shadow of the puppetmaster out of sight.

Making the theater

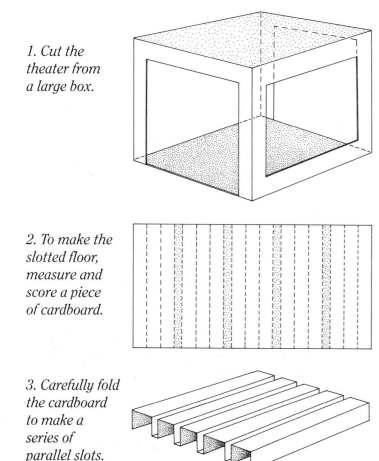

1. Cut the theater from a large box.

2. To make the slotted floor, measure and score a piece of cardboard.

3. Carefully fold the cardboard to make a series of parallel slots.

Collecting Materials

It is a simple matter to set up a theater and make puppets. The main material you need is plenty of scrap cardboard of different thicknesses. The theater is made from a large, strong cardboard box. The scenery and puppets are made from thinner cardboard that can be painted.

Planning the Story Line

Before you make the puppets and design the scenery, you will need to decide on a story line for a play. Write an outline, keeping your ideas very simple. Two scenes and four characters will be sufficient. You can only operate two puppets at a time single-handed.

Making the Theater

Cut the front and sides out of a large cardboard box, as shown here. The puppets slide along in slots in the stage floor. To make the floor, find a piece of thin cardboard and cut it to the same width as the theater. Score and fold the card as shown, making a series of parallel slots in the card. Make sure the wooden dowels that are attached to the puppets fit into the slots and move freely.

Finally, paint the theater and decorate it with colored paper scraps or wrapping paper.

Puppet Characters

Sketch the puppet shapes on paper before drawing them onto cardboard. These puppets are always seen in profile, so make sure that some of your characters are designed to enter from the left and others from the right.

Paint the puppets, cut them out, and then glue them onto lengths of wooden dowel. Make pieces of scenery from cardboard and position them in the slots.

The puppet theater

Puppet characters

Glue the puppets onto lengths of wooden dowel.

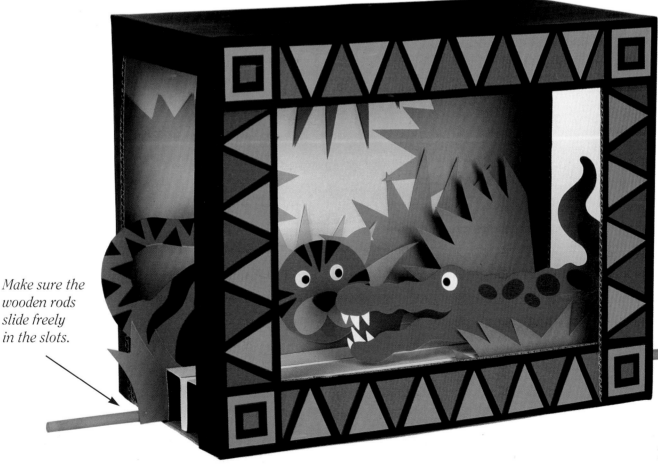

Make sure the wooden rods slide freely in the slots.

Junk Toys

Children at Play

Toys made from salvaged objects and materials are familiar in Africa today. In Botswana, they are now produced for export. Often, the name of the original manufacturer is still visible on the finished toy. Strangely, this adds to the value. There are many African children who make toys from discarded objects, because no other toys are available. In Kenya footballs are sometimes made out of plastic bags bound into a ball shape with string.

Automatons

Jointed toys became popular in Europe during the eighteenth century. By the nineteenth century they had become more complicated and were operated in a number of ways. The coiled spring was the most common method used. When the nineteenth century came to an end, the mass-produced, tin-plate toy industry was underway. Moving toys have been popular with children ever since. The majority of today's toys are made from plastic and are battery-powered.

Robot Automaton

This simple moving toy is made up of various shapes cut from plastic scraps. A snap fastened at each joint allows it to move freely. Use plastic that is rigid, yet thin enough for holes to be punched through to make the joints.

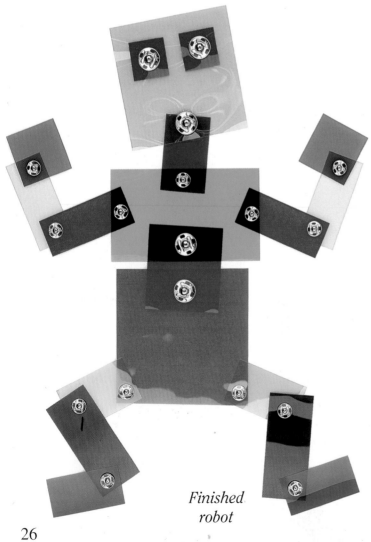

Finished robot

Punch holes in plastic pieces.

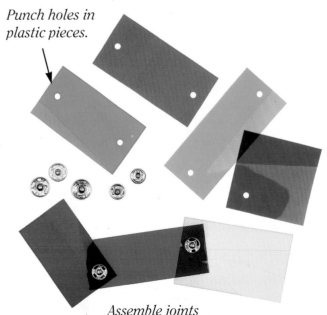

Assemble joints with large snaps.

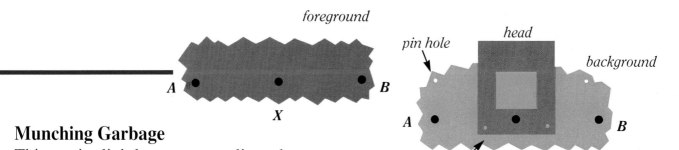
foreground

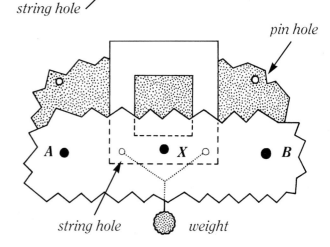

Munching Garbage

This toy is slightly more complicated and moves on a pivot, called a fulcrum. Cut the main pieces from strong, scrap cardboard. Paint or cover them with a collage of paper, foil, and plastic scraps. Make holes in the pieces, as shown.

Fix a weight to the head with two lengths of string. Attach the head to the background at point X using a split pin. Make sure the pin moves freely. Assemble the foreground and background pieces at points A and B, using split pins. Pin the "garbage dump" to a wall, swing the weight, and see the robot munch away.

Assembling the garbage dump monster

Garbage dump monster

swinging weight

27

Moving Wheels

Moving Around

You can create movement by building a system of interlocking cogs and wheels out of salvaged materials. Movement is transferred from one part of the machine to the next. A small cog interlocking with a large cog turns more frequently. These wheels do not move along. They simply turn around and around. Cog wheels can be seen inside old mechanical clocks and watches.

Cogs and Wheels from Junk

Collect together a variety of circular junk items, such as shallow cheese containers and lids of different sizes. Glue lengths of lollipop sticks to each cog as shown here. Make a hole through the center of each cog, then attach them to a cardboard base. Make sure the cogs rotate freely and the spokes interlock. When one cog is turned, all the others should move as well.

Moving cogs and wheels

Making the cogs

Glue sticks firmly to lid.

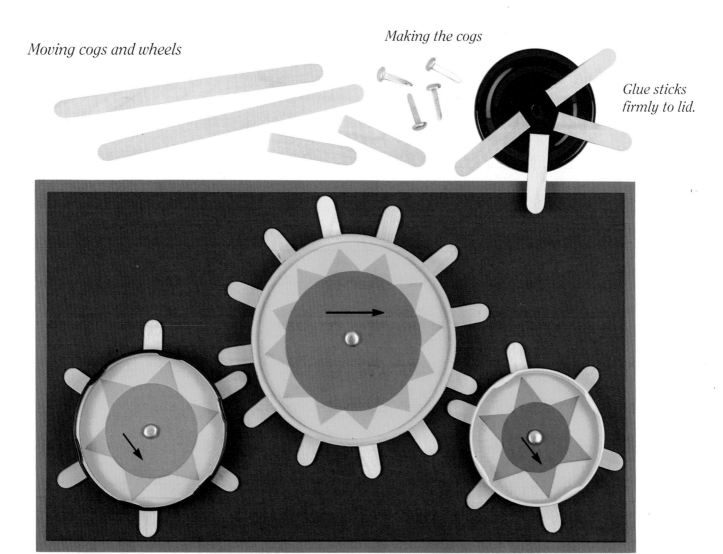

Moving Along

Here is an idea for making a three-dimensional machine that will move along a surface when pushed or pulled. This time you will need to collect together an even number of small plastic lids that are all the same size.

Making a Rolling Bug

Find or make a long, narrow box about 8 inches by 4 inches by 1.25 inches. Make a series of small holes along each side of the box—one hole for each pair of wheels. Use wooden kebob sticks for axles and thread them through the holes.

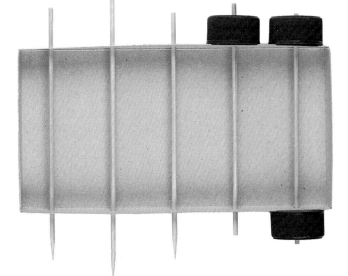

Assembling the wheels and axles

Make a hole in the center of each lid. Push them onto the axle, cutting off any extra length. Secure each lid to its axle with a drop of glue. Attach a length of string to the front of the box to pull it along. Make sure it moves smoothly on the wheels.

Decorate the box with scraps of plastic, colored paper, and yarn and turn it into a rolling bug.

Rolling bug

Glossary

Aborigines An ancient people who lived in Australia long before it was discovered by Europeans.

automaton A machine that operates automatically.

axle A bar or shaft connecting the wheels on a vehicle.

biodegradable A material that decomposes naturally.

cuttings Small sections cut from plant stems that form their own roots in water or soil.

dowel A small length of wood used to join two other pieces of wood together.

ecosystem The interaction between living things within their environment.

fulcrum The pivot about which a lever turns.

gourds Fruit of plants of the cucumber family. In Africa, dried shells were often used to make musical instruments and other artifacts.

graphics The art of drawing to mathematical principles.

gravel A mixture of rock fragments and pebbles.

humid A moist, damp atmosphere.

journal A written daily record in book form.

junk Discarded objects.

labeling Paper, cardboard, or another material attached to an object in order to identify it.

landfill sites Large pits that are filled with alternate layers of garbage and earth.

methane gas A colorless, odorless, flammable gas that can be used as a fuel.

monoprint A repeating pattern created with a unique printing block.

packaging Wrappings and boxes made specially to hold and protect retail items.

Picasso, Pablo Ruiz (1881–1973) A Spanish artist who is looked on by many people as the most inventive and innovative artist of the twentieth century.

portfolio A flat case used to store and carry papers.

propagate To grow new plants and cuttings.

rattans The stems of a climbing palm used for wickerwork and cane.

seedlings Young plants grown from seed.

shantytown Part of a town or city where poor people live in ramshackle huts often built from discarded materials.

More Information

Further Reading

Bawden, Juliet. *Fun with Fabric*. New York: Random House Books for Young Readers, 1993.

James, Barbara. *Waste and Recycling*. Conserving Our World. Milwaukee: Raintree Steck-Vaughn, 1990.

Javna, John. *Fifty Simple Things Kids Can Do to Save the Earth*. Kansas City, MO: Andrews & McMeel, 1990.

Lancaster, John. *Fabric Art*. Fresh Start. New York: Franklin Watts, 1991.

Morley, Jacqueline. *Clothes: For Work, Play & Display*. Timelines. New York: Franklin Watts, 1992.

O'Reilly, Suzie. *Knitting and Crochet*. Arts & Crafts. New York: Thomson Learning, 1994.

O'Reilly, Suzie. *Weaving*. Arts & Crafts. New York: Thomson Learning, 1993.

Stocks, Sue. *Collage*. First Arts and Crafts. New York: Thomson Learning, 1994.

Sources for Special Materials

Thrift stores, tag sales, and the remnant sections of fabric and craft stores are all good places to find fabric for the crafts in this book.

Addresses for Information

Center for Marine Conservation
1725 Desales Street NW, Suite 500
Washington, DC 20036

Environmental Protection Agency
Public Information Center
Washington, DC 20460

Environmental Defense Fund
257 Park Avenue South
New York, NY 10010

Friends of the Earth
218 D Street SE
Washington, DC 20003

Greenpeace
1436 U Street NW
Washington, DC 20009

National Wildlife Federation
1400 16th Street NW
Washington, DC 20036

The Nature Conservancy
1436 North Lynn Street
Arlington, VA 22209

Rainforest Action Network
300 Broadway, Suite 28
San Francisco, CA 94133

Index